Yvonne Brill
and Satellite Propulsion

By Ellen Labrecque

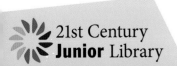

21st Century
Junior Library

Published in the United States of America by
Cherry Lake Publishing
Ann Arbor, Michigan
www.cherrylakepublishing.com

Content Adviser: Amelia Wenk Gotwals, Ph.D., Associate Professor of Science Education, Michigan State University
Reading Adviser: Marla Conn MS, Ed., Literacy specialist, Read-Ability, Inc.

Photo Credits: © Cristi Matei/Shutterstock Images, cover; © NASA/ Johnson Space Center, 4; © Harris & Ewing/Library of Congress, 6; © Esther Bubley/Library of Congress, 8; © NASA/ Goddard Space Flight Center, 10; © Yvonne Brill (US3807657)/ United States Patent and Trademark Office, 12; © NASA, 14; © Win McNamee/Staff/Getty Images, 16; © NASA/JPL-Caltech/ MSSS, 18; © NASA/Dan Casper, 20

Library of Congress Cataloging-in-Publication Data
Names: Labrecque, Ellen, author.
Title: Yvonne Brill and satellite propulsion / by Ellen Labrecque.
Description: Ann Arbor, MI : Cherry Lake Publishing, [2017] | Series: 21st century junior library. Women innovators |
    Audience: K to grade 3.
Identifiers: LCCN 2016029708| ISBN 9781634721844 (hardcover) | ISBN 9781634723169 (pbk.) |
    ISBN 9781634722506 (pdf) | ISBN 9781634723824 (ebook)
Subjects: LCSH: Brill, Yvonne Madelaine, 1924-2013–Juvenile literature. | Artificial satellites–Propulsion systems–
    Juvenile literature. | Women engineers–Biography–Juvenile literature. | Engineers–Biography–Juvenile literature. |
    Women inventors–Biography–Juvenile literature. | Inventors–Biography–Juvenile literature. | Outer space–
    Exploration–Biography–Juvenile literature.
Classification: LCC TA157.5 .L33 2017 | DDC 629.43/4092 [B] –dc23
LC record available at https://lccn.loc.gov/2016029708

Cherry Lake Publishing would like to acknowledge the work of The Partnership for 21st Century Skills.
Please visit *www.p21.org* for more information.

Printed in the United States of America
Corporate Graphics

CONTENTS

The National Aeronautics and Space Administration (NASA)
has been working on space exploration since 1958.

A Woman

We live in the space age. Spaceships rocket around the earth. Spaceships have landed on the Moon. One day, people could even take a spaceship to the planet Mars!

Yvonne Brill was a rocket scientist who helped make space travel happen. She **invented** ways to send and keep rockets in space!

Adventurous women like Amelia Earhart were important
role models for young girls like Yvonne.

Yvonne Madelaine Claeys was born on December 30, 1924, in Manitoba, Canada. Her mom and dad were **immigrants** from Belgium. Her dad worked as a **carpenter**. Yvonne was inspired by Amelia Earhart, a famous female pilot. Earhart was the first woman to fly solo across the Atlantic and Pacific Oceans. Yvonne wanted to do exciting things, too.

When Yvonne was growing up, the few women who studied science typically became chemists, not engineers.

Yvonne went to the University of Manitoba. She wanted to study **engineering**. But the school would not let her. They thought women weren't supposed to study engineering. So she studied **chemistry** and math instead. She graduated in 1945.

Early American rocket scientists were almost all men.

After college, she worked for the Douglas Aircraft Company in California. She worked on the first designs for an American **satellite**. At the time, she was the only woman rocket scientist working in the United States!

Create!

Create a new design for a spaceship. What would it look like? How would it work? Where would it be able to go?

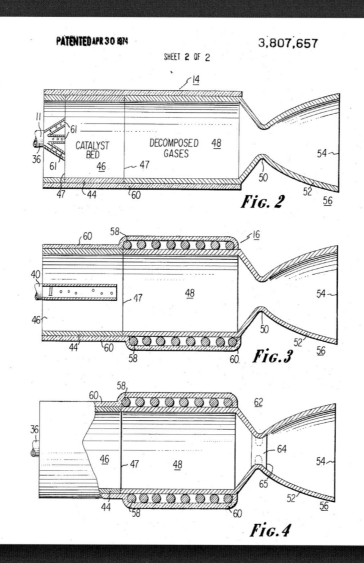

Fig. 2

Fig. 3

Fig. 4

To get a patent, Brill made detailed
drawings of her invention.

An Idea

In 1951, Yvonne married William Brill. The couple moved to Princeton, New Jersey. Yvonne worked for a new rocket-building company. In 1972, she **patented** a system to **propel** objects forward. The rocket **thruster** she invented helped keep satellites from slipping out of their **orbit**.

Global positioning system (GPS) satellites allow you to use digital maps in your car and on your phone.

Brill's invention also helped satellites use less fuel. They could stay in space longer without refueling. In the years that followed, Brill continued to work on propulsion systems. Her thrusters even helped NASA explore the Moon and study Mars!

Ask Questions!

Ask your teacher or librarian to tell you more about what satellites do. How many kinds are there? Did you know they can send radio and cell phone signals from space?

Brill received the National Medal of Technology and Innovation at a special ceremony.

A Legacy

In 2010, Brill was inducted into the National Inventors Hall of Fame. In 2011, U.S. president Barack Obama awarded her the National Medal of Technology and Innovation. Obama said her work "inspires us all to reach higher and try harder." Brill died in 2013. She was 88.

Mars is similar to Earth in many ways. NASA hopes
to send humans to live there by 2030.

Yvonne Brill's **legacy** is that her thruster is still used to propel rockets and satellites today. Humans have not visited Mars yet. But perhaps her invention will soon help us to do so!

Think!

If you had the chance to live on Mars, do you think you would go? Why or why not?

Brill encouraged other women to pursue exciting careers in engineering and science.

Exploring space is an exciting job. Yvonne Brill spent her life helping scientists do this. She was the first American woman rocket scientist. She was also one of the world's most important rocket scientists. Just like Amelia Earhart, Brill filled her life with exciting discoveries.

GLOSSARY

carpenter (KAHR-puhn-ter) a person who builds or fixes things using wood

chemistry (KEM-uh-stree) the scientific study of substances, what they are composed of, and how they react with each other

engineering (en-juh-NEER-ing) the study of how things, such as bridges and buildings, are built and constructed

immigrants (IM-ih-gruhnts) people who move from one country to another and settle there

invented (in-VENT-id) created something new from imagination

legacy (LEG-uh-see) something handed down from one generation to another

orbit (OR-bit) the curved path of an object around a planet like the sun or the earth

patented (PAT-uhn-tid) obtained the right from the government to use or sell an invention for a certain number of years

propel (pruh-PEL) to drive or cause to move forward

satellite (SAT-uh-lite) a spacecraft that is sent into orbit around Earth and can be used to study weather or to send electronic signals to Earth that run TVs, computers, and phones

thruster (THRUHST-er) a small rocket engine on a spacecraft

FIND OUT MORE

BOOKS

Gilliland, Ben. *Rocket Science for the Rest of Us*. New York: DK Books, 2015.

Hargittai, Magdolna. *Women Scientists: Reflections, Challenges, and Breaking Boundaries*. New York: Oxford University Press, 2015.

Swaby, Rachel. *Headstrong: 52 Women Who Changed Science—and the World*. New York: Broadway Books, 2015.

WEB SITES

Kids Astronomy
www.kidsastronomy.com
Find out more about outer space.

NASA—Jet Propulsion Laboratory
www.jpl.nasa.gov/education/BuildMissionGame.cfm?skipIntro=true
Explore this site and build your own space mission.

INDEX

ABOUT THE AUTHOR

Ellen Labrecque is a freelance writer living in Yardley, Pennsylvania. Previously, she was a senior editor at Sports Illustrated Kids. Ellen loves to travel and then learn about new places and people that she can write about in her books.